Questions and Answers: Countries

A Question and Answer Book

by Fran Hodgkins

Consultant:
Colin M. MacLachlan
John Christy Barr Distinguished Professor of History
Tulane University
New Orleans, Louisiana

Mankato, Minnesota

Fact Finders is published by Capstone Press
151 Good Counsel Drive, P.O. Box 669, Mankato, Minnesota 56002
www.capstonepress.com

Printed in the United States of America

Library of Congress Cataloging-in-Publication Data
Hodgkins, Fran, 1964–
Mexico: a question and answer book / by Fran Hodgkins.
p. cm.—(Fact finders. Questions and answers: countries)
Includes bibliographical references and index.
Contents: Where is Mexico?—When did Mexico become a country?—What type of government does Mexico have?—What kind of housing does Mexico have?—What are Mexico's forms of transportation?—What are Mexico's major industries?—What is school like in Mexico?—What are Mexico's favorite sports and games?—What are the traditional art forms in Mexico?—What major holidays do people in Mexico celebrate?—What are the traditional foods of Mexico?—What is family life like in Mexico.
ISBN-13: 978-0-7368-2479-8 (hardcover)
ISBN-10: 0-7368-2479-0 (hardcover)
ISBN-13: 978-1-4296-0220-4 (softcover pbk.)
ISBN-10: 1-4296-0220-1 (softcover pbk.)
1. Mexico—Juvenile literature. [1. Mexico.] I. Title. II. Series.
F1208.5.H63 2005b
972—dc22 2004021863

Editorial Credits

Megan Schoeneberger, editor; Kia Adams, series designer; Jennifer Bergstrom, book designer; maps.com, map illustrator; Wanda Winch, photo researcher; Scott Thoms, photo editor; Eric Kudalis, product planning editor

Photo Credits

Art Resource, NY/Schalkwijk, 6; Bruce Coleman Inc./Masha Nordbye, 12–13; Capstone Press Archives, 29 (top); Corbis/AFP, 8 (left); Corbis/Alison Wright, 18–19; Corbis/Archivo Iconografico, S.A., 7; Corbis/Danny Lehman, 11, 15, 16–17, 22–23; Corbis/Randy Faris, 8–9; Corbis/Royalty Free, cover (background); Corel, 1; Cory Langley, 20, 25; Doranne Jacobson, 27; Index Stock Imagery/Jerry Koontz, cover (foreground); Maxine Cass, 21; StockHaus Limited, 29 (bottom); Tom Till, 4

Artistic Effects

Chocolate Manufacturers Association, 24; Photodisc, 12 (left); Photodisc/Jules Frazier, 18 (left); Photodisc/Siede Preis, 16 (left)

1 2 3 4 5 6 10 09 08 07 06 05

Table of Contents

Features

Where is Mexico?

Mexico is south of the United States. It is almost three times the size of the U.S. state of Texas.

Two **peninsulas** stick out from the main part of Mexico. Baja California stretches into the Pacific Ocean. The Yucatán Peninsula is on the southeastern edge of the Gulf of Mexico.

The Sierra Madre Occidental mountain range stands in western Mexico. ➧

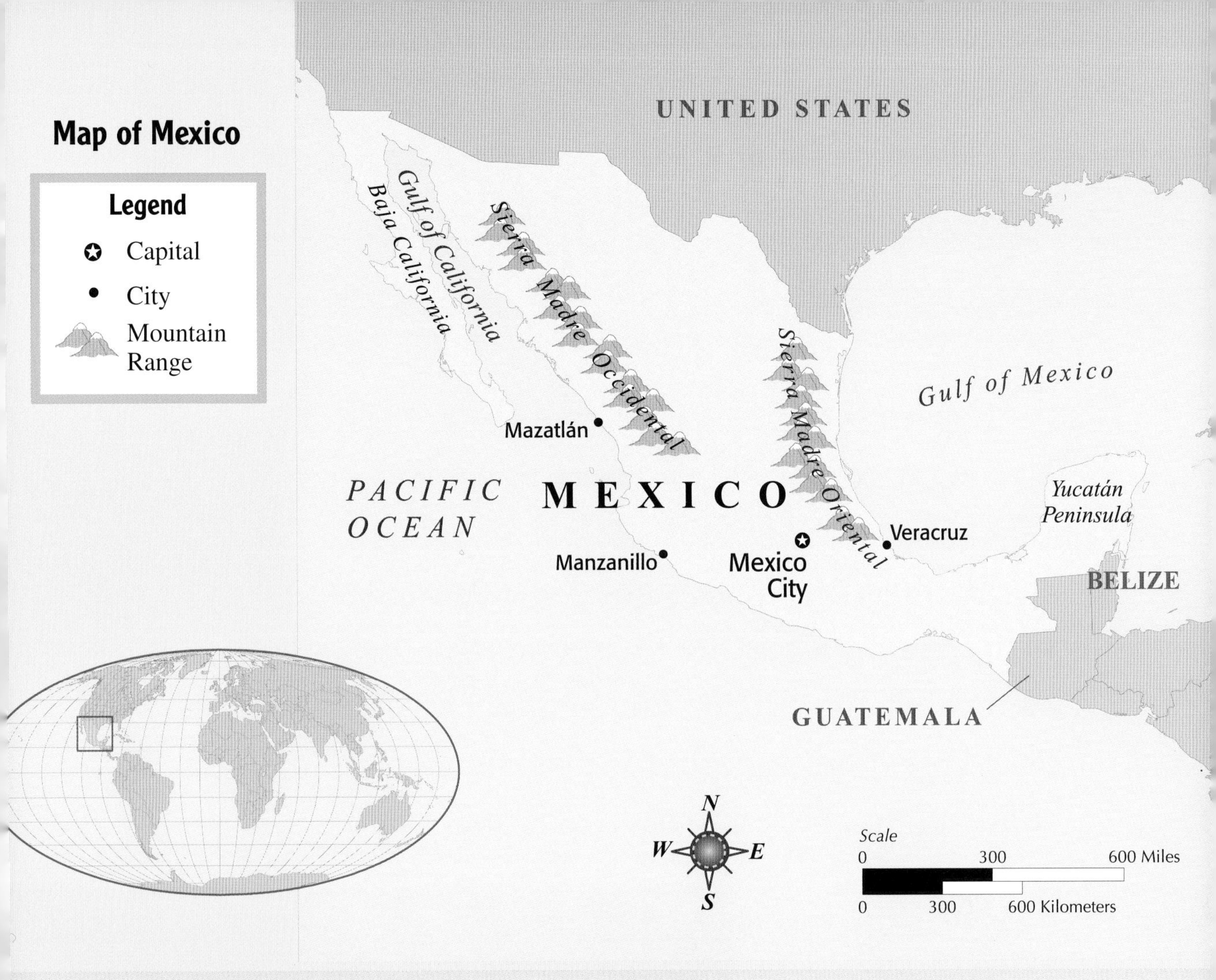

Mexico has many landforms. Mexico's central **plateau** is an area of high land. Two mountain ranges line the plateau. They are the Sierra Madre Occidental and the Sierra Madre Oriental. Southern Mexico has thick, wet **rain forests**.

When did Mexico become a country?

Mexico became its own country in 1821. It won its freedom from Spain. Spain had ruled Mexico since 1521.

By the early 1800s, some Mexicans felt that Spain was treating them unfairly. On September 16, 1810, Father Miguel Hidalgo asked Mexicans to fight for their freedom from Spain. The fight lasted 11 years.

Father Miguel Hidalgo (center, wearing black) encouraged Mexicans to fight for their freedom from Spain. ➧

Mexicans celebrated the Treaty of Córdoba, which ended Spain's rule over Mexico.

The Spanish signed the **Treaty** of Córdoba in 1821. This treaty freed Mexico from Spanish rule. In 1822, Agustin de Iturbide named himself **emperor**. But he was not a good leader. In 1823, Guadalupe Victoria became Mexico's first president.

What type of government does Mexico have?

Mexico is a **federal republic**. The United States also has this type of government. In a federal republic, a group of states is united under a president. Mexico has 31 states. Each state elects its own leaders. The states can make their own laws.

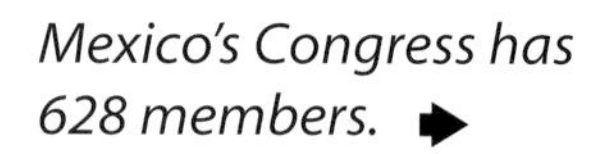

Mexico's Congress has 628 members.

The National Palace stands in Mexico City. Lawmakers use the building for special events.

Mexicans vote for their president. The president works with Mexico's Congress to make laws. Congress is made up of two parts, the Chamber of the Senate and the Chamber of Representatives. Congress meets in Mexico City, the capital of Mexico.

What kind of housing does Mexico have?

Most Mexicans live in cities. Large cities have high-rise apartment buildings and family homes. The homes are made of stone or **adobe**. Many Mexican homes have an outdoor walled garden. Plants and vines fill the garden.

Where do people in Mexico live?

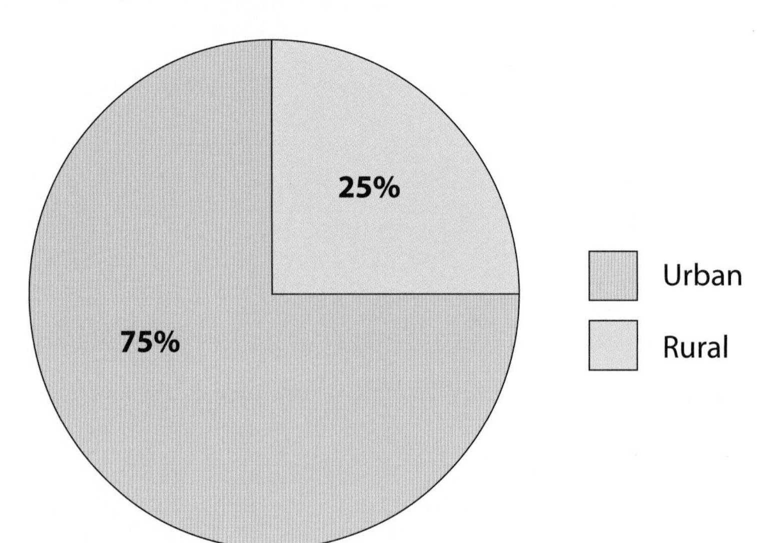

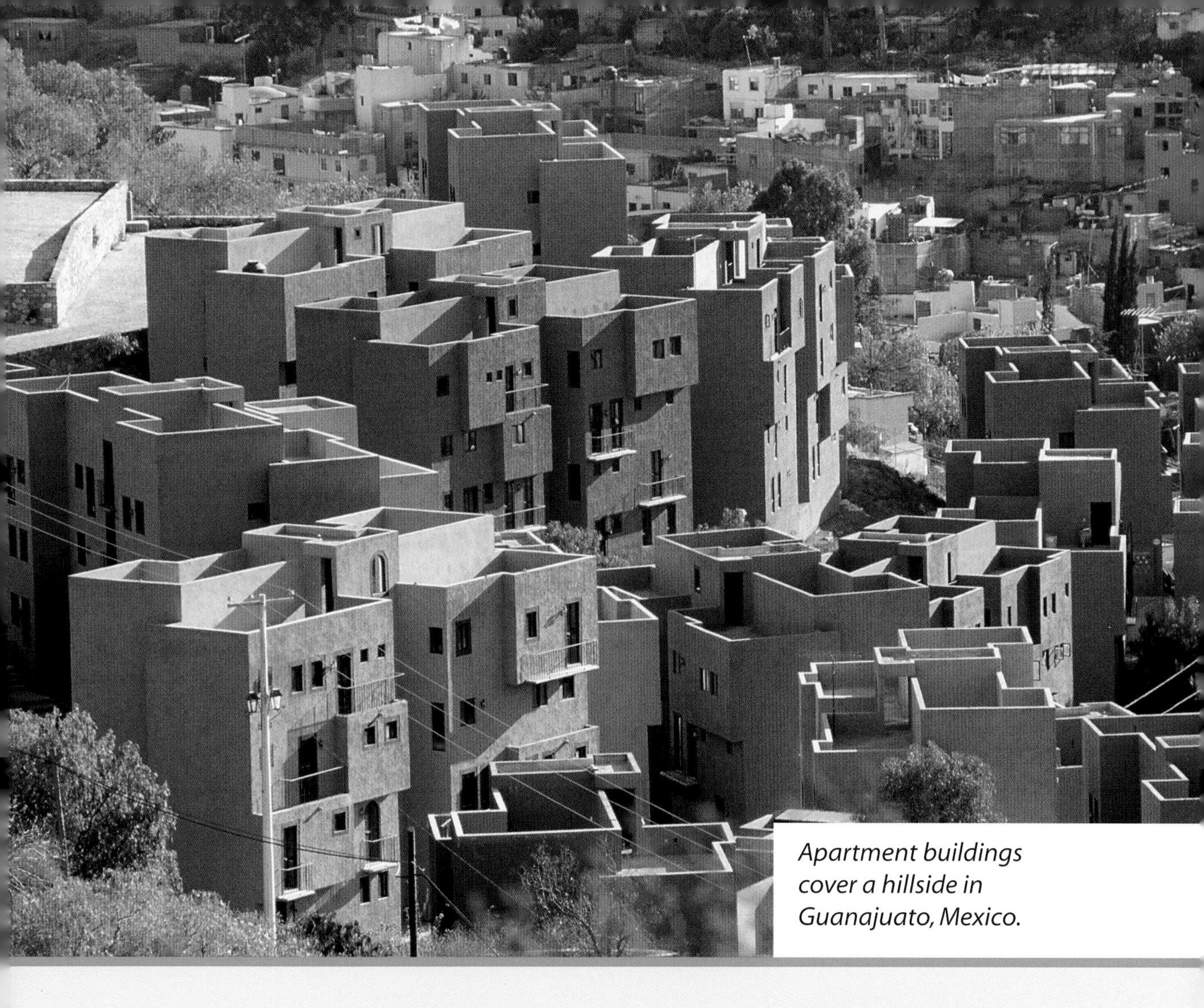

Apartment buildings cover a hillside in Guanajuato, Mexico.

Other Mexicans live in small houses in the countryside. These houses have dirt floors and few windows. They are made of adobe, clay, bricks, or stone. They have flat roofs of red tile or sheet metal.

What are Mexico's forms of transportation?

Mexico has highways that link big cities and towns. Most highways are in the center of the country. Trucks carrying goods travel on the highways.

In cities, car traffic is heavy. People often ride buses or taxis. Mexico City and Guadalajara have subways.

Fact!

In the country, some farmers use donkeys and cattle to carry their goods to market.

Green taxis fill a busy street in Mexico City.

Many cities also have airports. Airplanes carry people from Mexico to places around the world.

Ships carry goods and people. **Ports** for ships include the coast cities of Veracruz, Mazatlán, and Manzanillo.

What are Mexico's major industries?

Most Mexicans work in service businesses. Tourism is one of these businesses. Millions of people visit Mexico every year.

Many Mexican businesses make products. Mexico's factories make cars, trucks, clothes, rubber, and paper. Some factories make cars, computers, and stereos for U.S. companies.

What does Mexico import and export?

Imports	*Exports*
aircraft	*manufactured goods*
electrical equipment	*oil*
machinery	*silver*

Workers in a Mexican factory build a car for a U.S. company.

Farmers in Mexico grow crops and raise animals. Crops include cotton, sugarcane, coffee, and corn. Farmers in southern Mexico grow **cacao** for making chocolate. Farmers also raise cattle, turkeys, chickens, and hogs.

What is school like in Mexico?

All Mexican children from age 6 to 14 must go to school. After kindergarten, children go to an elementary school for six years. They then start basic secondary school. This school is like middle school in the United States. After three years, students go on to upper secondary school. This school is like U.S. high school.

Fact!

Mexico's government gives free textbooks to every student in public school.

Mexican classrooms are often crowded with students.

Mexico's public schools are crowded. Many schools have two shifts. Some students go to class from 8:00 in the morning until 12:30 in the afternoon. Other students have class from 2:00 in the afternoon until 6:00 in the evening.

What are Mexico's favorite sports and games?

Soccer and baseball are the most popular sports of Mexico. Mexicans often play these games wherever they can find space. Many pro baseball and soccer teams play in Mexico.

Mexicans also enjoy a sport called *charrería.* This sport is like a rodeo. Horse riders compete in different events. In one event, a rider throws a rope to catch a horse by the back legs. In another event, a rider catches a bull by its tail. The rider tries to pull the bull to the ground.

Fact!

Mexico's soccer team has been to the World Cup finals 12 times, but they have never won the championship.

A bullfighter holds a red cape in front of a charging bull.

Bullfighting also is popular in Mexico. In a bullfight, a **matador** faces a bull in a bullring. He waves a cape to get the bull to charge toward him. He stabs the bull with spears. The matador usually kills the bull by the end of the fight.

What are the traditional art forms in Mexico?

Mexican artists make pottery, clay figures, and woven blankets. Artists often use bright colors and designs. They sell their work at markets.

Many famous painters have come from Mexico. Diego Rivera created large mural paintings on walls. Frida Kahlo painted many self-portraits.

Mexican artists make clay vases and other pottery to sell at markets. ➡

Diego Rivera's murals are large and colorful.

People all over the world enjoy reading Mexican stories and poems. Poet Octavio Paz was the first Mexican to win a Nobel Prize for writing. Laura Esquivel wrote the book *Like Water for Chocolate.* This book was made into a movie.

What major holidays do people in Mexico celebrate?

Mexicans celebrate the Day of the Dead at the beginning of November. Families bring flowers and food to the graves of their loved ones. Families sometimes have picnics at the graves.

September 16 is Mexican Independence Day. Every year, Mexicans honor Father Hidalgo's call for freedom. Church bells ring. People set off fireworks and wave flags in parades.

What other holidays do people in Mexico celebrate?

Christmas
Mexican Flag Day
New Year's Day
Semana Santa (Holy Week)
Valentine's Day

Mexicans cover the graves of their loved ones with flowers to honor them on the Day of the Dead.

People in Mexico also celebrate Cinco de Mayo. This holiday remembers May 5, 1862. On this day, Mexican soldiers won a battle against the French army. The French were trying to take over Mexico. The Mexican soldiers kept their country free.

What are the traditional foods of Mexico?

Tortillas made of corn or wheat are part of many Mexican dishes. Mexicans bake, fry, or grill the tortillas. They wrap cooked tortillas around beans, chicken, cheese, and other foods. Tacos, **flautas**, burritos, and enchiladas are all made with tortillas.

Some Mexican food gets flavor from peppers. Jalapeño peppers are very spicy. Serrano chile peppers are smaller than jalapeños and five times hotter.

Fact!

Ancient Mexicans were the first people to make chocolate. They roasted the seeds of the cacao tree with corn. They then ground the mixture into a powder. They added vanilla to the powder to make a chocolate paste.

Mexicans use tortillas to make many kinds of food.

Tamales are a favorite Mexican food. To make them, Mexicans steam cornmeal dough in a corn husk or banana peel. The cornmeal is often mixed with chicken or pork. Some people even make tamales with chocolate.

What is family life like in Mexico?

In Mexico, two families often live in the same home. Parents sometimes share their home with their married son or daughter. Other family members may also live in the home. Shared homes often have kitchens for each family.

What are the ethnic backgrounds of people in Mexico?

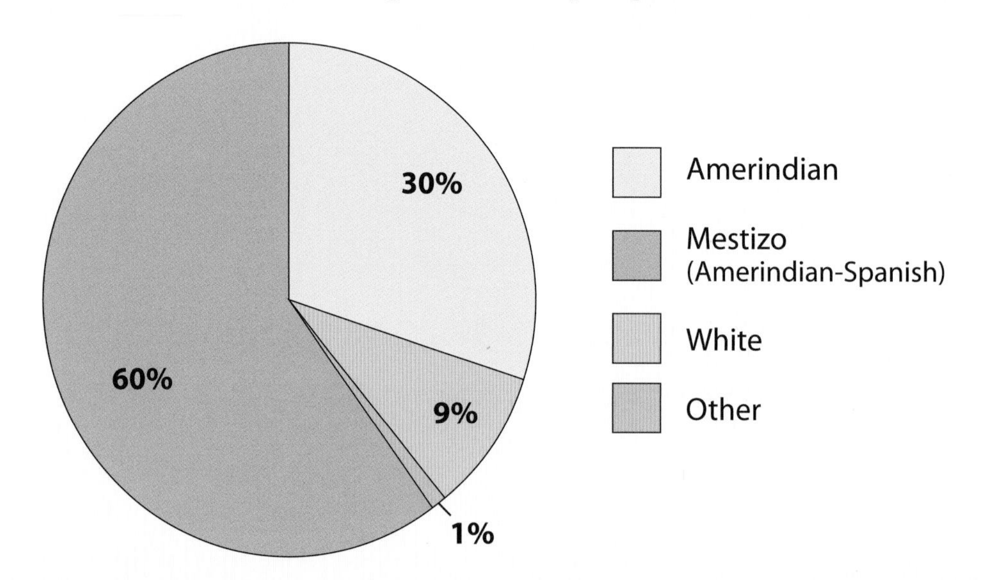

In Mexico, grandparents often live with their grandchildren.

Godparents are another part of Mexican families. Parents choose godparents shortly after their child is born. Friends or family members are chosen to be godparents. They take a special interest in their godchild and help in many ways.

Mexico Fast Facts

Official name:

United Mexican States

Land area:

742,486 square miles (1,923,040 square kilometers)

Average annual precipitation:

25 inches (63.5 centimeters)

Average January temperature:

70 degrees Fahrenheit (21 degrees Celsius)

Average July temperature:

74 degrees Fahrenheit (23 degrees Celsius)

Population:

104,907,991 people

Capital city:

Mexico City

Language:

Spanish

Natural resources:

copper, petroleum, salt, silver

Religions:

Roman Catholic	*89%*
Protestant	*6%*
Other	*5%*

Money and Flag

Money:

Mexican money is called the Mexican peso. In 2004, 1 U.S. dollar equaled 10.8 pesos. One Canadian dollar equaled about 8.4 pesos.

Flag:

The Mexican flag has three stripes. The stripes are green, white, and red. The coat of arms is in the middle of the white band.

Learn to Speak Spanish

People in Mexico speak Spanish. It is the official language. Learn to speak some Spanish using the words below.

English	*Spanish*	*Pronunciation*
hello	hola	(OH-lah)
good morning	buenos días	(BWAY-nohs DEE-ahs)
good-bye	adiós	(ah-dee-OHS)
please	por favor	(POR fah-VOR)
thank you	gracias	(GRAH-see-us)
boy	niño	(NEEN-yoh)
girl	niña	(NEEN-yah)

Glossary

adobe (uh-DOH-bee)—a brick made of clay mixed with straw and dried in the sun

cacao (kuh-KAW)—a tree that produces a seed from which cocoa and chocolate are made

emperor (EM-pur-ur)—the male ruler of an area called an empire

federal republic (FED-ur-uhl ri-PUB-lik)—a government of many states led by a president or prime minister with officials elected by the voters

flauta (FLOU-tuh)—a tortilla wrapped around a filling and deep-fried

godparent (GOD-pair-uhnt)—someone who promises his or her support for a child when the child is baptized into the Christian religion

matador (MAT-uh-dor)—a bullfighter

peninsula (puh-NIN-suh-luh)—a piece of land that is surrounded by water on three sides

plateau (pla-TOH)—an area of high, flat land

port (PORT)—a harbor or place where boats and ships can dock or anchor safely

rain forest (RAYN FOR-est)—a tropical woodland that gets at least 100 inches (254 centimeters) of rain each year

treaty (TREE-tee)—an official agreement between two or more groups or countries

Internet Sites

FactHound offers a safe, fun way to find Internet sites related to this book. All of the sites on FactHound have been researched by our staff.

Here's how:

1. Visit *www.facthound.com*
2. Type in this special code **0736824790** for age-appropriate sites. Or enter a search word related to this book for a more general search.
3. Click on the **Fetch It** button.

FactHound will fetch the best sites for you!

Read More

Asher, Sandy. *Mexico.* Discovering Cultures. Tarrytown, N.Y.: Benchmark Books, 2003.

Auch, Alison. *Welcome to Mexico.* Spyglass Books. Minneapolis: Compass Point Books, 2003.

DeAngelis, Gina. *Mexico.* Many Cultures, One World. Mankato, Minn.: Blue Earth Books, 2003.

Winter, Jonah. *Frida.* New York: Arthur A. Levine Books, 2002.

Index